HEROES OF
THE RAF

GW00467521

No 43 SQUADRON

Leonard James

Bretwalda Books Ltd

First Published 2012
Copyright © Leonard James 2012

All rights reserved. No reproduction of any part of this
publication is permitted without the prior written
permission of the publisher:

Bretwalda Books
Unit 8, Fir Tree Close, Epsom,
Surrey KT17 3LD

info@BretwaldaBooks.com

To receive an e-catalogue of our complete
range of books send an email to
info@BretwaldaBooks.com

ISBN 978-1-907791-37-6

Bretwalda Books Ltd

Introduction

When I was a small boy my father gave me a set of cigarette cards. He had been in the RAF during the War and like all small boys in the 1960s I made Airfix Spitfires and watched movies such as Angels One Five on television. So I pored over the cigarette cards, read the potted squadron histories on the back and stuck them all into a scrapbook.

There was one card that puzzled me. It showed what I took to be a

chicken. I knew all about chickens because my Great Aunt Hilda kept a few in her large rural garden. I just could not work out why any heroic RAF squadron would want a chicken as their official badge. It was a puzzle I could not solve. Years later I realised that what I had taken to be a chicken was a fighting cock – and a most worthy symbol it was for the squadron concerned. No.43 has long been one of the RAF's premier squadrons, and its longevity is as impressive as its combat record.

No.43 has been formed, disbanded and reformed several times since it was established in 1916. Most recently it was stood down on 13 July 2009, though there are plans to reform it as a Typhoon Eurofighter squadron. Given the parlous state of the nation's finances as I write this there is some doubt if the new squadron will form as expected. We shall see. What cannot be doubted is the glorious history of the squadron, its men and machines.

HAWKER HURRICANES, 1939
In 1939, No.43 Squadron was equipped with Hawker Hurricane fighters. The Hurricane was the most numerous fighter in RAF service at the time as it combined rugged construciton, heavy armament and low cost – always a consideration in peace time.

PLAYER'S CIGARETTES

No. 43 (FIGHTER) SQUADRON, R.A.F.

THE FIGHTING COCK, 1926
The cigarette card that the author was given as a boy. It shows the squadron badge of No.43 Squadron, a gamecock and not a chicken as he at first thought. The badge was officially adopted in 1926, at a time when most RAF squadrons and bases were acquiring badges and mottoes.

The
Great War

O n 15 April 1916 the Royal Flying Corps base at Stirling, Scotland, was home to No.18 Reserve Squadron. The squadron, in common with most reserve and training units at the time, was equipped with a bewildering variety of aircraft types. But the RFC, like all branches of the British Army, was then gearing up for the widely expected "big push" that everyone expected in the summer of 1916. That was to take the form of the Battle of the Somme, during which the RFC would establish and maintain air superiority over the British section of the Western Front, driving the Germans from the skies over the trench systems.

It was clear that every man and machine was going to be needed and the orders went out for an expansion of the RFC. No.18 Reserve Squadron was therefore converted to be No.43 Squadron of the RFC. For the time being the mixture of aircraft was retained, but as the autumn became the winter, No.43 Squadron was re-equipped with a scout (or fighter) aircraft called the Sopwith 1½ strutter.

By this date the various roles of military aircraft were becoming fairly well established. When aircraft had first gone to war in 1914 they had been used exclusively as reconnaissance or scout aircraft. The pilots had flown out ahead of the ground armies to try to spot enemy troops, then flew back to base to make their reports. Within months some pilots began dropping explosive devices, soon to be dubbed bombs, or shot at other aircraft in the hope of bringing them down. By late 1916 there were specialist bomber aircraft, while two seater reconnaissance aircraft with radios were spotting for artillery and seeking out enemy ground formations and structures. As the assorted tasks were taken up by specialist aircraft and squadrons, the original scout squadrons were gradually left with the task of attacking enemy aircraft and became de facto fighter squadrons, though they generally continued to be termed scouts.

The Sopwith 1½ strutter had been designed in December 1915 to be a long range, offensive patrol scout with the ability to carry a few light bombs in case some useful target was spotted by the pilot. The aircraft was officially named the Land Clerget Tractor, but gained its ubiquitous nickname from the layout of the struts that joined and braced the upper and lower wings. The aircraft had large fuel tanks, that gave it the ability to stay in the air for almost four hours, then a very good time indeed, and so to penetrate far beyond German lines.

The key feature of the aircraft was its armament. The pilot sat at the front, just behind the engine and operated a .303in Vickers machine gun that shot forwards through the arc of the propeller. Some of the early interrupter gears

---

SOPWITH 1½ STRUTTER, 1917
This two-seater fighter and scout entered service in the spring of 1916 and continued to see front line service until October 1917 when it was withdrawn to secondary theatres and rear-area duties. It ended its days in the early 1920s as a trainer.

did not work terribly well and it was not unusual for a Sopwith pilot to shoot his own propeller off. Behind the pilot sat an observer in a separate cockpit. He was armed with a .303in Lewis machine gun that was attached to the then revolutionary scarf ring fitting that allowed the observer to swing his gun quickly and easily through a wide arc, making his fire nimble and effective.

In January 1917 No.43 Squadron moved out to France with their Sopwiths and entered combat. One of the men of No.43 was not destined to stay with the squadron for very long. Captain Alan Scott was one of the worst pilots in the squadron. During training he crashed more than any other student, and managed to break both his legs. Nevertheless, he persevered and qualified as a pilot. Despite his lack of skill, he proved to be an inspired leader of men and was soon a flight commander. He proved to be particularly talented at navigation and so was sent on missions to photograph locations behind German lines. He shot down three German aircraft with No.43, then was shot down himself but walked away from the crash uninjured. In March he was given command of No.60 Squadron and left No.43. He was shot down again in July and this time wounded badly enough to be sent back to Britain. He then took up a pilot training post - with one of his pupils being Winston Churchill. Scott survived the war, but died in the 1920s.

On 7 March the squadron welcomed to its ranks a man who managed to combine being a newly qualified pilot with having already shot down 10 German aircraft. Frederick Libby was an American from Colorado who had volunteered to be an ambulance driver in the Canadian Army when World War I broke out. In 1916 he tired of his medical role and instead volunteered for the RFC. He trained as an air gunner, and it was while flying as a gunner that he shot down his 10 Germans. He thus became the first American "ace" of all time. Having qualified as a pilot, Libby was posted to No.43 Squadron where he shot down two more aircraft. When the USA joined the war, Libby was transferred to the US Army and went back to America to train new aircrew, give morale boosting talks and join the Liberty Loan drive. He often said, when training air gunners, that "Aerial gunnery is 90 percent instinct and 10 percent aim." After the war Libby went into the oil business and he survived until 1970.

Unfortunately in the spring of 1917 the Germans re-equipped their squadrons with Albatros D.II and D.III fighters that were fast, agile and armed with twin forward firing machine guns. Not only did they have a technological edge over the RFC aircraft, but the Germans had reorganised

CAPTAIN ALAN SCOTT, 1917
Born in New Zealand, Scott went to France with No.43 Squadron and was awarded the Military Cross for his activities photographing German positions when under heavy anti-aircraft fire. At this date the RFC had no specific medals of its own, so its officers and men were awarded army medals.

their air service with specialist Jagdstaffeln (hunter squadrons) equipped and trained to destroy Allied aircraft. The Jagdstaffeln, or Jastas, proved to be horribly effective and the result was "Bloody April" when the RFC lost 245 aircraft and the Germans only 66. British losses eased when offensive missions across the front lines were halted, but that ceded control of the air to the Germans.

One of the very few high profile German casualties during Bloody April was Sebastian Festner, an Albatros D.III pilot who had shot down 12 British aircraft in a combat career lasting three months. He was shot down by Lt Joseph Dickson of No.43 Squadron near Gavrelle.

No.43 Squadron took its share of the losses during Bloody April, but there were some survivors. Among these was Henry Forrest, an Australian who had joined the RFC after serving with the ANZACs at Gallipoli. Forrest fought his way through Bloody April as he had done through Gallipoli with dash and courage. He was then shot down and badly injured on 6 August. He seems to have learned his lesson, however, for when he returned to combat with No.2 Squadron in February 1918 he began a steady toll on German aircraft that continued to the end of the war, by which time he had shot down 11 aircraft. After the war he returned to Broken Hill in New South Wales, got married and led a quiet life until his death in the 1950s.

SOPWITH CAMEL, 1917
The astonishing agility of the Sopwith Camel made
it lethal in combat. Camel pilots shot down a
confirmed 1,294 enemy aircraft, more than was
claimed by any other type of aircraft. It entered
service in June 1917 and remained in combat up to
the Armistice.

Another of the founder members of No.43 Squadron who managed to
survive the turbulent days of Bloody April was the Yorkshireman Lt John
Womersley. He had already shot down an early Albatros fighter, but during
this time with No.43 shot down two more Albatros fighters and a pair of
DFW CV reconnaissance two seaters. He left the squadron in December
1917.

Also surviving from the original squadron members was an observer
named Frank Gorringe, a Canadian who had volunteered for the army on the
day he heard that Britain had declared war. Gorringe had a quiet time with
No.43, attracting no official notice either good or bad. However he later
retrained as a pilot and went on to shoot down 14 enemy aircraft. After the
war he returned to Canada and to his more placid career as a railway official.

By July 1917, No.43 had been given the duties of short-range, high-speed bombing raids. It was at this time that the squadron was joined by Captain Harold Balfour, who shot down two German aircraft in his Sopwith 1½ Strutter before he was himself shot down and injured. After a few months training new pilots in Britain, Balfour returned to No.43 Squadron to find that they had in September 1917 received the famous Sopwith Camel scout aircraft. The squadron's fortunes changed dramatically. It abandoned bombing raids for ground attack and close army support missions, hitting forward German positions with accuracy and reliability.

Balfour quickly shot down another seven Germans and was promoted to Major. Gifted as he was in combat, it was recognised that Balfour was a superlative instructor so he was once again moved to a training squadron, this time as the commanding officer. His attitude to air warfare was summed up when he said " "We were too busy fighting to worry about the business of clever tactics." After the war he entered the Air Ministry as a civil servant, then was elected to Parliament for Thanet in 1929. His Parliamentary career was marked by his waspish turn of phrase. He served as a junior minister in the Air Ministry in World War II and became Baron Balfour when he left the House of Commons at the 1945 election. He died in 1988.

The Sopwith Camel was meanwhile quickly becoming the most famous British aircraft of the Great War. The Camel was a single seat scout with twin .303in Vickers machine guns firing forward through the propeller arc. It had a top speed of 115mph and ceiling of 21,000 feet. Neither of these was exceptional in 1917, but the manoeuvrabiltiy of the Camel put it in a class of its own. The engine, fuel tank, pilot and guns were all crammed into the front 7 feet of the fuselage, which gave the Camel some rather bizarre (and often alarming) flying characteristics. It could turn to the right almost three times quicker than any other aircraft, and could lose height in a nose-down spin much quicker than any other fighter. In the hands of a skilled pilot, the Camel was almost unbeatable in the air. The fictional Great War ace Biggles was given a Camel for his daring exploits. Unfortunately the Camel was unforgiving and a good number of pilots were killed when learning to fly it.

Arriving with No.43 Squadron alongside the Camel was an unprepossessing Essex man, Lieutenant Cecil King. King had served in the Essex Regiment for two years, but had now joined the RFC and within three weeks of joining No.43 Squadron he drove down a German fighter. It was a good opening, but thereafter King spent several months without any success at all. Then in February 1918, King seemed to find his pace. He shot down four German aircraft that month, and three more in March. His tally thereafter climbed rapidly. He remained with No.43 Squadron until the end of the war, finishing with a total of 19 kills to his credit.

Rather less successful was Lt Gerard Crole, who joined No.43 from No.40 Squadron with a fine reputation as a fighting pilot and a string of five confirmed kills to his credit. Perhaps because he was more accustomed to the Nieuport fighter than the Camel, Crole had barely joined No.43 before he was shot down by the German ace Fritz Rumey near Marcoing and captured. After the war, Crole gave up flying entirely in favour of a career as a lawyer.

The cheerful South African Lt Hector Daniel joined No.43 Squadron on 26 November 1917, just four days after Crole was shot down. Daniel downed his first German on 17 February near Pont a Vendin, then shot down a second at almost the same place on 9 March. In the weeks that followed, Daniel developed a real flair and appetite for aggressive patrol tactics – "He has displayed the greatest skill, keenness and courage in aerial fighting", wrote his commanding officer of him. On 12 April Daniel was on morning patrol near La Gorgue when he spotted a pair of German Albatross D.V fighters. At the time this was the newest and most feared German fighter, which was faster and more nimble than the D.III that it replaced. Daniel was not put off by the reputation of the new fighter and pounced. Both German aircraft went down within minutes of each other. After lunch, Daniel went up again. This time he was some miles north east of La Gorgue when he saw another D.V. Again he attacked and again the German was shot down.

Daniel ended his career with No.43 with nine confirmed kills. He then went back to South Africa where he joined the South African Air Force (SAAF) as a career officer. He eventually rose to the rank of Brigadier and spent World War II as Director of Air and Technical Services in the SAAF.

Arriving with No.43 Squadron in January 1918 was Lt Geoffrey Bailey, who had joined the RFC in 1917 straight from Westminster School. Bailey quickly earned the nickname of "Lumpy", though it is not clear why. He shot down his first enemy aircraft 16 February when he downed an Albatros D.III over Henin. By the time the war ended he had built his score up to eight confirmed kills.

Serving alongside Bailey was George Lingham who had joined No.43 before Christmas and shot down his first German aircraft on 9 March near Pont a Vendin. Over the months that followed, Lingham shot down five more enemy aircraft, one of them a Fokker Dr.I triplane, a famously agile dogfighter. He survived the war and went on to lead the Heston Aircraft Company, one of the most successful British manufacturers of aircraft components during the inter war years.

When the great German offensives of March and April struck, the British army was thrown back in confusion. Only the constant harrying attacks of No.43 Squadron and other RFC units served to disrupt the German supply lines and so slow down the advance of the grey-clad hordes enough for the British Army to reform its front and halt the dangerous attacks. Amid the battlefield crisis, the RFC was reorganised into a new force entirely separate

DFW C.V, 1917
The German two-seater reconnaissance aircraft C.V, manufactured by DFW, entered service in 1917 with Germany and Bulgaria and remained in action to the Armistice. In all 3,250 were built and several remained in use into the 1920s as private aircraft.

CAPTAIN H. W. WOOLLETT, 1917
Woollett came to No.43
Squadron having already shot
down five German aircraft with
No.24 Squadron. He ended the
war with 35 kills of aircraft and
balloons. After the war he
remained in the RAF, tutoring
one Douglas Bader in No.23
Squadron, and left the services in
1945.

from the army that had given it birth. The new Royal Air Force (RAF) was
under the redoubtable Sir Hugh Trenchard, one of the key proponents of air
power in the early 20th century.

Throughout these months, No.43 Squadron was home to one of the more
colourful characters ever to fly with the RFC. Captain Henry Woollett was
aged 23 when he joined the squadron in March 1918. He had already
acquired an impressive reputation as a fighting pilot, having shot down the
required five enemy aircraft to gain the informal designation of "ace". He
was a distinctive figure in his leopard skin flying helmet and gauntlets, and his
aircraft was equally noticeable having a dragon painted down the side of its
fuselage. He began his career in No.43 Squadron with a bang, shooting down
10 aircraft before the end of March.

On 12 April he took to the skies in his distinctive Camel and before the
sun set that day he had shot down six German aircraft. A contemporary pilot
wrote "Captain H.W. Woollett of No. 43 Squadron...whilst leading a patrol,
he saw a German machine, out-manoeuvred it, fired about thirty rounds and
saw it spin down and crash. During this fight he had been attacked by several
other machines. Without delay he climbed rapidly above his attackers and
dived on to a two-seater, firing as he went, causing this machine also to crash.

Once again he out-climbed his opponents, looped away from two attacking Fokkers, made a vertical bank, and again dived on the tail of an Albatross. After he had fired about 40 rounds, this machine burst into flames and fell to pieces. He then went home. At 5 p.m. the same evening he attacked thirteen enemy aircraft.... He first fired 30 rounds into one of the enemy aeroplanes, which turned over on its back and fell to pieces. He then climbed again, manoeuvred rapidly among the remaining twelve machines, avoiding the fire of his opponents until he could fire a burst into an Albatros, which spun down and crashed. He then made for home. On crossing the lines he saw another enemy machine above him. Once more the climb of his 'bus enabled him to get over his enemy, and he crashed his sixth machine for the day."

Woollett went on to shoot down four more aircraft and three observation balloons with No.43 Squadron before he crashed his Camel and was sent home to Britain. There he took up a position with a training squadron, where he ended the war. His total score was 36, made up of 25 aircraft and 11 balloons. He had been awarded the DSO, the Military Cross and Bar and the French Legion D'Honneur.

A second American served with No.43 at this time. This was the young Henry Clay of Missouri. He had volunteered for the American Signal Corps, but had been passed on to the RFC for training as a pilot. He served with No.43 Squadron for several weeks to gain experience of combat flying before transferring back to American service to pass on what he had learned. He shot down eight German aircraft over the Western Front in the summer of 1918 and survived the war to join the US occupation forces, based at Koblenz. He died in the 1919 influenza epidemic.

Also with No.43 Squadron during the German advances of March and April was Captain John Trollope. Trollope had worked his way up from the ranks in the Royal Engineers, before transferring to the RFC in the summer of 1916. He flew with No.70 Squadron until he moved to No.43 in January 1918. On 24 March the British army was in headlong retreat on a 40 mile front as the first of the great German offensives of spring 1918 burst forward near St Quentin. Trollope went up into a sky swarming with enemy aircraft and in the space of 9 hours of fighting managed to shoot down seven of them.

Four days later, Trollope led a nine aircraft patrol back into the skies, but this time luck was not with him. The patrol was bounced by Jasta 52 with its Albatros fighters. Trollope was shot down, but not before accounting for three German aircraft.

The News of the World reported his efforts as follows:

"How a British boy-airman brought down six Hun aeroplanes in one day during two flights behind the enemy lines has just been revealed. Unfortunately, the 20-year-old hero of the adventure, Capt. John L. Trollope, R.F.C., is now officially reported missing, exactly a week after his day of victories. He was last seen by his squadron commander "fighting hard over the enemy lines." The record feat of destroying the six Hun aeroplanes was accomplished on March 21, the day that the Germans launched their hate bolt against the British lines. Capt. Trollope's modest account of the day's work hardly gives a just impression of the hazards and odds which he overcame in order to surpass the previous record bag of five Hun machines in one day. In a letter to his mother, Mrs. Howard W. Trollope, of Green Hayes, Banstead, Surrey, written on the evening of his triumphs, he wrote simply:

'This has been the most wonderful day of my life. I myself have destroyed six Hun machines—three this morning and three this afternoon. The first this morning I shot to pieces, and it broke up in mid-air; the second went down in flames—both of them two-seaters. The third, a single-seater, which literally exploded in mid-air and fell in pieces. Then I saw two two-seaters quite low down, which I crashed. After this I saw one of our fellows attacked by 12 Huns. I went up to him and let him get away, but ran out of ammunition, so returned to the squadron.'

This is all Capt. Trollope made of the episode. Other accounts, however, show that the airman was at times engaged with several hostile machines at the same time. On one occasion he met a party of three of the enemy trying to cross the battle-line. In the middle of the engagement his machine-gun jammed, and he had to draw off. The moment his gun was going again he closed once more with his opponents, the nearest of whom was attacked at point-blank range. This was one of the machines which "fell in pieces." Since returning to the front last January the gallant airman had brought down 18 enemy machines. Six machines down in a day is believed to be a record, the best achievement hitherto standing to the credit of the late Capt. Albert Ball, V.C., who once brought down five Huns in one day. Capt. Trollope, who is the younger son of the late Howard Trollope, of Westminster, was a despatch-rider in France during 1915, and only took up flying during the autumn of 1916. Within a few weeks of qualifying he was out in France. Only recently he became a champion air fighter. He was educated at Banstead Hall, and left Malvern College to join the Army. His elder brother is abroad with the Queen's Westminsters. Mrs. Trollope said that there is

AIR COMBAT, 1918
An illustration from a contemporary magazine
shows an aerial combat over the Western Front in
1918. The German aircraft is shown having
crumpled up in mid-air. The relatively fragile wood
and canvas construction of World War I aircraft
made this a not unusual occurrence if bullets
damaged a main supporting strut.

hope that her son is alive, as a strong west wind was blowing on the day that he
failed to return, and it is thought that he may have landed safely behind the
enemy lines owing to engine trouble."

Trollope was, indeed, alive – though far from well. He managed to get his
Sopwith down in one piece, but the German doctors found his left arm
smashed below the elbow and had to amputate his hand. He was later
repatriated to Britain through the Red Cross. He survived until 1958.

Shot down at the same time as Trollope was Lieutenant Robert Owen,
who had been credited with seven kills. His time in captivity was enlivened
by repeated escape attempts. He managed to get away from his captors three
times, but was recaptured on the first two occasions. On his third attempt,

FRIEDRICHSHAFEN G3
This mighty German bomber entered service early
in 1917, and 338 were built before the war ended.
After the war surviving aircraft were had the rear
gunner's position removed and replaced with a
fully-enclosed passenger cabin to become a
medium-range airliner.

Owen managed to get to Danzig (now Gdansk in Poland) and stowed away
on a ship heading for neutral Norway. He subsequently made his way across
the North Sea and arrived unannounced at his home in Newcastle, giving his
mother a great shock when he walked into her kitchen. Owen went on to
serve with the RAF in World War II as a medical officer.

Among the replacements brought into No.43 Squadron to make up such
losses was Captain Charles Chaplin Banks, who had seen extensive service in
the trenches before joining the RFC. Banks had gained his first two names
as homage to the British actor Charles Chaplin, father of the rather more
famous Charles Chaplin who went to the USA to become a movie star. He
had previously been with No.44 Squadron defending London from German
bombers. There he had been the first man to force down intact a German
Gotha bomber, allowing this huge aircraft to be studied by British scientists.

Banks opened his score with No.43 Squadron on 6 April and over the
following six weeks downed four more German aircraft. On 31 May he

achieved a first for any British pilot. He was on patrol near Monchy when he spotted a Friedrickshafen G. This was a brand new type of German heavy bomber able to carry a ton of bombs, then a remarkable achievement. As well as the usual gunner positioned behind the pilot, the Friedrickshafen G had a gunner seated in the nose, making this a particularly hazardous aircraft to attack. Banks did not hesitate, but swooped to the attack and swiftly knocked out the bomber's engines. He escorted the crippled bomber to the ground, ensuring that yet another German type was available for study.

In August No.43 began to be re-equipped with Sopwith Snipes. These single seat scouts were designed specifically to match the German fighters at higher altitudes, taking on roles of attacking German aircraft and protecting British bombers on raids behind German lines. Conversion to the aircraft was completed in September, and No.43 Squadron entered combat once again.

Arriving with the squadron at about the same time as the Snipe was an already established "ace", George Howsam MC. After a few days with No.43 he shot down a Fokker DVIII, thus bringing his tally up to eight Germans shot down and five driven down. It was his last victory. After the war, Howsam returned to his native Canada to join the new RCAF. He spent most of World War II as Director of Training, then retired in 1945.

Fighting alongside Howsam was Captain Augustus Orlebar, who had gained fame in March 1918 when he shot down Lothar von Richthofen (brother of the rather more famous Baron Manfred von Richthofen, "The Red Baron"). Orelbar shot down only one aircraft during his time with No.43, a Fokker DVII shot down over Remaucourt on 29 Septeber 1918. This brought his tally to eight. After the war, Orlebar remained in the RAF, taking part in the service air racing team that competed for the Schneider Trophy. He was on the staff of Fighter Command when World War II broke out and served as a senior staff officer until his sudden death from natural causes in 1943.

The most successful No.43 pilot on the Snipe proved to be Captain Banks. On 27 September he downed a Fokker DVII at Cambrai, then shot down a second Fokker at Quiercy four days later. On 30 October, as the war drew a close he shot down a third Fokker at Aulnoye. Banks thus ended the war with a total of 13 kills. He was awarded a Military Cross (MC) and a Distinguished Flying Cross (DFC) during his combat career.

In 1946 Banks was to be presented with a George Cross by King George

CAPTAIN AUGUSTUS ORLEBAR, 1918
Although he gained fame first with the RFC and then the RAF, Orlebar began his military career with the Bedfordshire Regiment in 1915. He was wounded by a sniper in Gallipoli and spent almost a year out of action before going to France as an RFC pilot. He was to be wounded twice more before the arrival of peace.

VI, that medal was not awarded to Banks himself but to his son Arthur Banks who fought as a fighter pilot in World War II before being shot down over Italy and joining the partisans. The younger Banks fought with the patisans behind German lines for five months before he was captured by the Germans. They tortured him for some days, but Banks refused to give them any information about his guerrilla group. The Germans then handed Banks over to the Brigate Nere, the hard core fascists who were still supporting Mussolini as the war drew to a close. They executed the younger Banks without trial. The killers were arrested after the war and imprisoned for 20 years.

The Great War ended in November, so the squadron's combat career in Snipes was limited.

No.43 Squadron was then moved into Germany as part of the British army of occupation, and in August 1919 came back to Britain to be stationed at RAF Grantham in Lincolnshire. On 31 December 1919 the squadron was, along with many others, disbanded. The first incarnation of No.43 Squadron was over.

Off to War

After the end of the Great War in 1918, the newly founded RAF was almost abolished, the task of flying aircraft being returned to the army. But it found a role for itself out in the Empire. The majority of troublesome tribes in more remote areas had long relied on the rugged and

GLOSTER GAMECOCK, 1926
Only 108 Gamecocks were ever built due to a high crash rate, no fewer than 22 being lost in landing accidents in three years. Despite this the Gamecock was a fast and manoeuvrable fighter that was notable for being one of the first to have internally-mounted machine guns.

inaccessible terrain in which they lived to evade or ambush forces sent against them, but aircraft negated such advantages. In 1920 Islamic fundamentalists rose in a rebellion of holy war in Somaliland. A British expeditionary force was sent out, accompanied by 12 D.H.9 bombers, which had been hastily converted to act as air ambulances as well as bombers. So well did the D.H.9s perform that the government decided to expand the RAF for colonial purposes. This new emphasis had an effect on aircraft design, with a need for easy maintenance in foreign climes and the ability to take off from short, often bumpy runways.

As a result No.43 Squadron was reformed at RAF Henlow in Bedfordshire, and given back its old Snipes. In 1926 the squadron re-equipped with Gloster Gamecocks, a single seat, biplane fighter armed with twin .303 Vickers machine guns. It was this aircraft that inspired the squadron badge of a

HAWKER FURY, 1932
This No.43 Squadron aircraft is a Hawker Fury that boasts the chequerboard markings that by this date had become traditional for the squadron. The Fury entered RAF service in 1931 and remained with front-line squadrons until January 1939 when it was replaced by the Hawker Hurricane.

fighting gamecock, since it was at this date that RAF squadrons first started acquiring formal badges. The aircraft did not last long, however, due to reliability problems and in 1928 it was replaced by the Armstrong Whitworth Siskin. The Siskin looked like another unremarkable biplane, but was in fact the first all-metal frame aircraft to be provided to the RAF in numbers. The Siskin was astonishingly agile, and so was beloved by spectators at air shows and formed the main display aircraft of the RAF for some years.

In 1930 the squadron gained a new commander in the shape of Sqdn Ldr Leonard Slater, already a distinguished pilot who had shot down six German aircraft in World War I. Slater spent two years commanding the squadron before moving to become the senior air officer on the carrier HMS Courageous. He went on to hold a number of senior command positions, retiring in 1949 with the rank of Air Marshal.

Despite its advantages, the Siskin lasted little longer than the Gamecock and in 1931 was replaced by the famous Hawker Fury. The Fury was to be the most important inter-war fighter of the RAF. It was sleek and agile, with an impressive top speed of 223mph and a ceiling of 29,500 feet. It was the first fighter to exceed 200mph when fully loaded and had excellent agility in the air. No.43 Squadron was lucky to get the Fury. Defence spending cuts meant that most fighter squadrons got the cheaper, but less effective Bristol Bulldog instead.

Good as the Fury was, the Hawker company knew that it could do better. In 1934 the Air Ministry finally changed its procurment policy from one based on fighting colonial campaigns from rough, poorly equipped airfields to one anticipating a major European war fought from permanent, quality air bases. Hawker could finally produce a sophisticated and quality fighter. Their chief designer Sidney Camm took all the lessons learned in building the various models of Fury and produced the Hurricane. This fighter was rugged, dependable, easy to fly and cheap – so the Air Ministry ordered it in large numbes. No.43 was re-equipped with Hurricanes in November 1938. Only just in time as it turned out.

The Hurricane was a low-winged monoplane fighter with the cockpit set high up to give the pilot excellent all round vision. It was equipped with eight .303 machine guns, an armament then considered to be eccentrically heavy at a time when most fighters had two or four guns. It had a top speed of 324mph and a range of 600 miles while being able to reach 34,000 feet. The wings were of advanced metal-skinned construction, though the fuselage was more conventional fabric over metal struts. The air frame was built specificallly to take the Rolls Royce Merlin engine, which powered a variable pitch propeller.

At the time the Hurricane was first built the RAF envisaged a war against Germany being fought in France with static trench systems, much as the Great War had been fought. The French had earmarked a variety of private and commercial airfields for the use of the RAF in wartime and the Hurricane was designated to be the fighter sent over to France to operate from these smaller, but well equipped airfields. The considerably more sophisticated and more expensive Spitfire was to be kept in Britain to defend British cities against the Luftwaffe.

Despite this division of labour between the two RAF fighters, No.43

HAWKER HURRICANE, 1939

When war broke out in 1939, No.43 Squadron was equipped with Hawker Hurricanes, then the most numerous fighter in the RAF. The Hurricane had entered service in December 1937 and by 1939 was equipping 18 squadrons. It remained in service to the end of the war.

Squadron stayed at their home base of Tangmere, in Sussex, when war broke out on 3rd September 1939. It was the other Tangmere Hurricane squadron, No.1, that went to France. No.43 did not stay long, however, flying off to Acklington in Northumberland in November.

The commander of the squadron when war broke out was Sqdn Ldr Charles Lott, one of the older squadron commanders in the RAF at the time. He had joined the RAF in 1922 at the age of just 16, working as an Aircraft Apprentice at RAF Halton. Five years later he qualified as a pilot and in 1933 gained a commission as an officer. After a time on the intelligence staff in Iraq, Lott returned to flying duties with No.41 Squadron which was then flying Demons out of Aden, though they later returned to Britain to be equipped with Spitfires. He then moved to No.43 squadron where he began flying Hurricanes for the first time.

Another No.43 pilot who had worked his way up from the lowly occupation of Aircraft Apprentice was Frank Carey, who held the rank of Sergeant as the war broke out. He had joined the RAF in 1927, becoming a pilot in 1935 and joining No.43 in 1938. Unlike Lott, Carey had already seen combat having been engaged with a force of Heinkel HeIII bombers off the coast of Northumberland on 30 January. On that occasion he and another pilot shared the credit for shooting down one of the bombers. On 3 February he shared the credit for shooting down a second bomber and later than month gained his commission. He was awarded the Distinguished Flying Medal (DFM) for his victory on 3 February. The citation stated that his skill and aggression had been exemplary, especially given the low cloud and poor visibitliy during the action. Carey then left No.43 for No.3 Squadron, where he shot down another four German aircraft before being himself shot down over Belgium on 14 May.

A third pilot with No.43 who had worked his way up through the ranks was Sergeant Peter Ottewill, who had joined the RAF as a boy apprentice in 1931 at the age of 16. He graduated as a pilot in 1938 and joined No.43, staying with the squadron as war broke out. It was Ottewill who shared the bomber on 3 February with Carey and he went on to claim two more German bombers, one in March and one in May.

The German bomber downed on 3 February was shared with a third pilot, another man who had been in No.43 since before the war. Peter Townsend was a Flight Lieutenant at this date and the Heinkel for which he shared the credit was the first German aircraft to come down on British soil during the

FLIGHT LIEUTENANT PETER TOWNSEND, 1939 Townsend was a 25 year old regular officer with No.43 Squadron when the war broke out. He later served in Spitfires and in nightfighters as well as being commanding officer of a number of RAF bases. He ended the war as Equerry to King George VI and would later have a famous romance with Princess Margaret.

war. Next day Townsend and fellow pilot Caesar Hull took the trouble to go to see the injured German crew in hospital. He later kept in touch with one of them, Karl Missy, beginning a friendship that would last for life.

The months spent in northern England, Scotland and the Orkneys were tough and dangerous. The conditions in the bitter winter weather were dreadful as groundcrew and pilots struggled to keep aircraft flying in subzero temperaturs. Often the men had to hack ice off the wings before a Hurricane would fly. Several pilots took off to patrol the bleak waters of the northern seas and simply vanished – their fate unknown.

On 8 April a large force of German bombers was detected heading for the Royal Navy base of Scapa Flow on the Orkneys and No.43 was scrambled to intercept. It proved to be the beginning of a day long series of running fights as formations of Heinkel He111 bombers came in off the North Sea at different heights and from different directions hoping to catch the defences by surprise. One pair of pilots, Edmondson and Arbuthnot broke the RAF rule book by attacking the Heinkels head on at top speed. It was held in pre-war RAF manuals that the high closing speed of such an attack would make accurate shooting impossible, but Edmondson proved them wrong by pouring fire into a bomber until its port engine exploded and the aircraft fell into the sea.

Later that day Sergeant Herbert Hallowes (known to his mess mates as Darkie) was on patrol off Duncansby Head when he sighted two Heinkels.

Hallowes turned to attack, got into position above and behind the enemy aircraft and opened fire at 400 yards range. After just two seconds his guns jammed. In disgust, Hallowes veered off from the attack and turned for base at Wick. Hallowes came in to land on the runway. Much to the startled surprise of those men on the ground watching Hallowes land, he was followed by a Heinkel bomber calmly coming in to land on the runway behind the Hurricane.

It turned out to be the bomber at which Hallowes had fired his short burst. His shooting had been more accurate than he had thought and not only was the Heinkel in no position to make the long flight back to Germany, but two of the crew had been badly injured. The pilot had decided to follow the British fighter back to its base and land so as to ensure that his comrades received prompt medical aid.

Next day was a bright sunny day. A lone Heinkel was attacked by seven Hurricanes of No.43 Squadron. This time the Heinkel was so badly damaged that it clearly would never make land. Hull and Townsend watched it go down. The Heinkel landed heavily in the sea and three crew members were seen to scramble into a dinghy. Townsend circled overhead while Hull sent out a radio message calling up an air-sea rescue patrol boat. However, the Hurricanes were low on fuel and had to head for home before the rescue boat arrived. The boat never found the dinghy, and the Germans were presumed to have died. When the message came through to No.43 that the Germans

SERGEANT HERBERT HALLOWES, 1940
Throughout his time at No.43 Squadron, Hallowes was known as "Darkie" due to his dark complexion. In 1940 he achieved the almost unique distinction of being awarded a Distinguished Flying Medal and bar at the same time.

had not been rescued, Townsend stared bleakly out of the window at the gloriously sunny weather. "Today is too lovely a day for dying," he said and headed off alone to his quarters.

Townsend was then given command of his own squadron, No.85, which he led with conspicuous success throughout the Battle of Britain. He ended the war having been awarded a DFC and bar, and being highly thought of both professionally and socially. In 1944 he was appointed Equerry to King George VI. He later became famous for an ill-fated romance with Princess Margaret, after which he retired from royal service and became an author of non-fiction books, many on air related topics.

After many gruelling months up north, in May 1940 No.43 went back to Tangmere. The move was not accidental. The German panzers were swarming across northern France, smashing everything in their path. The German onslaught had begun on 10 May with armoured columns backed by infantry and artillery pushing deep into Belgium and the Netherlands. The Dutch capital fell to a daring paratroop landing and within hours the Germans were advancing rapidly. But impressive as these attacks were, they were only a feint. While the British and French armies moved northeast to aid the Belgians and Dutch, the main German attack was delivered further south through the Ardennes hills and over the key River Meuse at Sedan. Advancing on a narrow front, the German panzers smashed through the French defences, then raced west spreading destruction and confusion in their wake. The panzers moved fast, leaving the infantry to plod along behind and mop up disjointed and confused French units as they came.

The reason the German armoured units could move quickly, without waiting for infantry or artillery support, was that the Luftwaffe had achieved air superiority overhead. The panzers and pilots kept in touch by radio – an unheard of novelty – ensuring that wherever the panzers went, the Luftwaffe was always above them. The air war had begun at dawn on 10 May when German bombers, with large fighter escorts, hit the pre-war French military air bases. Not only were many aircraft destroyed on the ground, but most of the French repair and maintenance sheds were blasted to pieces. The RAF fighters in France escaped this early devastation by being based at what had been civilian airfields in pre-war days. But now that almost the full burden of war flying over France fell to them, the RAF fighters began to sustain heavy losses. The French begged Churchill to send more fighters to France. Churchill turned to Sir Hugh Dowding, head of Fighter Command. And

Dowding refused. He believed France was already finished and he would need all his squadrons to protect Britain.

Dowding was not alone. On 19 May Lord Gort, British commander on the continent, defied his French allies and orders from the British government. He too concluded the French were finished and was determined to get as many of his men home as possible. He ordered a retreat to the port of Dunkirk and asked the Royal Navy to take his men off the beaches while the RAF provided air cover.

43 SQUADRON AT TANGMERE, 1940
A photo of No.43 Squadron pilots at Tangemere with, among others, Hallowes (3rd from left) and Townsend (2nd from right). Although this photo has the date 1940 written on the reverse the pilots are standing in front of a Hurricane with a two-bladed propeller, a feature phased out by this date.

Arriving back at Tangmere in May, No.43 Squadron was still commanded by Sqdn Ldr Lott and flew straight into this maelstrom. Sortie after sortie, patrol after patrol was flown to the skies over Dunkirk. The fighters landed in Kent to refuel before setting off over the North Sea to give themselves the longest possible combat time over Dunkirk. The Squadron went on several sorties out to Dunkirk, penetrating as far as Abbeville and Amiens on occasion.

Several German air raids got through to Dunkirk, attacking the men on the beaches and bombing the ships off shore, but most were halted. In all 338,000 men (140,000 of the French or Belgian forces) were evacuated. The men had to leave all their heavy equipment behind, but it was trained men that Britain needed. After all, nobody doubted that the Germans would invade Britain next.

DUNKIRK BEACH, 1940
The evacuation of the British army, along with many Frenchemen, from Dunkirk was a triumph of combined operations involving the army, navy and air force. No.43 Squadron flew almost constant patrols to try to keep the Luftwaffe away from Dunkirk.

A few days after the end of the Dunkirk evacuation, No.43 welcomed back Frank Carey, now a Flight Commander sporting a DFC to add to the DFM he had been awarded when with No.43. After being shot down in Belgium, Carey had found himself dumped off at a semi-abandoned air field where other downed aircrew had been left. As the British Army fell back on Dunkirk, the RAF squadrons stationed in France were hurriedly evacuated before the panzers overran their bases and everyone in authority forgot about the handful of men at the abandoned airfield in Belgium.

Fortunately the base had an elderly, but still airworthy Bristol Bombay twin-engined transport aircraft. Carey and his fellow airmen fuelled it up, packed on board and took off. Carey acted as rear gunner on the trip keeping a wary eye open for prowling German fighters. By keeping low and flying as fast as the elderly aircraft could manage, the men succeeded in getting back to RAF Hendon. Carey reported for duty, only to find that he had been posted as missing presumed killed and was no longer on the books of No.3 Squadron. He therefore found himself sent back to No.43, which was short of a flight commander.

Over in France, the French had formed a defensive line along the Somme and the Aisne and were digging in to confront the expected renewed German onslaught. On 5 June the German assault began in the western section of the line, near Amiens. Two days later, on 7 June, the panzers broke through, crossing the Somme and streaming south and west toward Rouen and Paris. No.43 was sent to carry out a ground attack sweep on the columns of supply trucks and infantry pouring into the gap opened up by the panzers. Peter Ottewill was sent out on two sories. He shot down a Messerschmitt BF109 in the morning, then got a second when on a second sortie in the afternoon.

Turning for home, Ottewill was bounced by some German fighters. His Hurricane burst into flames and Ottewill was badly burned before he managed to get the canopy open and bale out. He came down in a hay field, where a French farmer quickly bundled him under a haystack as German soldiers were nearby. The farmer later pointed the injured Ottewill in the direction of the front lines and amazingly the downed pilot managed to make his way to safety, eluding the Germans. The French administered first aid, then passed Ottewill on to a retreating British unit, which was evacuated by sea to Southampton. From there Ottewill made his own way to Tangmere, walking into the Officers' Mess to be greeted by his astonished comrades who had seen his aircraft going down in flames and assumed he was dead.

Ottewill was taken off for treatment by Sir Harold Gillies, the father of plastic surgery, and was commissioned as an officer in 1941. No longer able to fly, Ottewill transferred to anti-aircraft gunnery (which organisationally was linked to Fighter Command as part of the air defence of Britain). In 1943 he was awarded the George Cross for resecuing the crew of a Beaufighter which had crashed on landing, skidding into the base's bombdump and catching fire. He later served in the Korean War, on the air staff in Washington DC and commanded RAF South Cerney. He retired in 1965 and took up farming. He died in 2003.

Ottewill was not the only No.43 pilot shot down in that hectic day of fighting over northern France. Sergeant Hallowes, who had led down the Heinkel in Scotland, was with No.43 when it encountered a formation of Messerschmitt Bf109 fighters. Hallowes got himself on the tail of a German and was about to fire when a stream of bulllets slammed into the cowling, knocking out his engine. Hallowes pulled his Hurricane out of the dogfight, turned its nose south and began gliding toward the ground in the hope that he would land safely behind French lines. Once again, however, bullets began peppering his aircraft. Realising it was too dangerous to stay where he was, Hallowes pulled back the cockpit canopy and began clambering out intending to jump by parachute. As he did so, however, the 109 that had been attacking him flashed past. Hallowes then dropped back into his seat and pressed the button that fired his guns, pouring a stream of bullets into the German fighter, which promptly burst into flames and went into a vertical dive out of control. Hallowes then jumped and landed by parachute. Unlike Ottewill he came down uninjured and safely within reach of a French army unit. He was soon back with No.43 in England.

When Hallowes was recommended for a much deserved DFM for his actions over France, it was realised that although he had shot down 21 enemy aircraft since the war began and had been in almost continual action he had not before been recommended for any recognition at all. Hurriedly catching up on their oversight, the RAF awarded him a DFM and bar together, the medals coming through on 6 September 1940.

Meanwhile, Hallowes was not the only No.43 Squadron pilot to have a lucky escape. Pilot Officer Charles Woods Scawen was sent up along with five other pilots of the squadron from Tangmere to intercept a formation of Germans heading for Portsmouth. The Hurricanes attacked in the standard tactic of two groups of three each in a V formation. The combat that followed

MESSERSCHMITT BF109B, 1940
The 109 was the main opponent of RAF Fighter Command in 1940, yet it was something of a mystery. Early models had only two machine guns, but by 1940 a number of other variants with a variety of guns and cannon were in service. The hefty punch of the cannon came as a shock to the RAF.

ended inconclusively, though Woods Scawen sent a Messerschmitt 110 down with smoke pouring from one engine. Most of the bombers got through, but their formation had been broken and the bombing was scattered.

Woods Scawen then found himself alone in the sky, separated from the rest of the squadron. He was at about 15,000 feet and over the Channel. He began to head north back to the English coast when he saw a formation of about 50 Junker Ju87 Stuka divebombers heading in the same direction. The Germans clearly thought they were alone for they were flying straight and level, something all combat pilots are warned not to do if enemy aircraft are about. Woods Scawen knew he had the element of surprise on his side and thought that if he attacked fast from behind he could rake the entire formation from end to end, then climb steeply away in front of the Germans, trusting to the superior climbing ability of the Hurricane to get him away from danger before the Germans could react.

Acting fast before he was spotted, Woods Scawen put his nose down and open the throttle to gain speed. As soon as he was within effective range of his guns he opened fire. One Stuka at once went into a dive with smoke pouring from the engine. Woods Scawen shifted his sights to a second Stuka, and saw that break off into a vicious spin. Closing on a third victim, Woods Scawen had his aim spoiled as his fighter hit the slipstream of the German bombers. On to a fourth Stuka he moved, and was gratified to see flames licking from its cowling. Then his own cockpit exploded into fragments as a German gunner poured an accurate burst of fire into the British fighter.

Woods Scawen found himself covered in fragments of canopy, and was alarmed to see his wings speckled with dozens of bullet holes. Then pain lanced through both his legs and he knew he had been hit. Woods Scawen pulled up the nose of his Hurricane to escape the formation of Stukas, but then found himself heading straight for a formation of Messerschmitt Bf110 fighters.

The new arrivals must have been flying as escort to the Stukas, but Woods Scawen had not seen them until now. Putting his nose back down, he accelerated away taking advantage of the 30mph difference in speed between a Hurricane and a Bf110.

Back at Tangmere, Wood Scawen was met by first aid teams who lifted him from his cockpit and loaded him on the ambulance for hurried transport to the Medical Officer. The MO carefully cut away the pilot's blood-soaked trousers and flying boots to reveal a mass of small puncture wounds. These were not, as Woods Scawen had feared, German bullets but a mass of tiny fragments that the German bullets had torn off the frame of the Hurricane. "You've got multiple foreign bodies in both legs," said the MO. Woods Scawen then burst out laughing both at relief that he had not stopped a bullet and at the thought of having foreign bodies in him. He was still laughing when his fellow pilots bought him a drink before packing him off to hospital.

Those "multiple foreign bodies" were considered to be a great joke by the men of No.43 squadron. The story was quickly spread through Fighter Command, and it appeared in the newspapers ten days later. Woods Scawen was back on duty a month later. Amazingly this was the sixth time that Woods-Scawen had been shot down since the war had begun, but only the first time that he had been injured. He had been shot down four times over Britain, and once over France during the Dunkirk campaign. Each time he had got back to Tangmere without serious mishap. His luck was not to last for sadly he was shot down and killed in September. Tragically his brother Philip was shot down and killed less than 24 hours later.

The Battle of Britain

T he Battle of Britain that followed was fought for control of the air over the English Channel. The German navy had suffered badly during the invasion of Norway and were wary of facing the Royal Navy. They would do so only, they said, if the Luftwaffe had control of the skies overhead. While the German army readied itself to invade, and the German navy prepared to transport them over the Channel, the Luftwaffe began the process of destroying the RAF.

INTELLIGENCE DEBRIEF, 1940

After every combat flight, RAF pilots had to submit a report that gave details of thier route and actions. If the base intelligence officer felt anything needed clarification or he wanted additional details he would call the pilots to a debriefing.

During July and early August the Luftwaffe concentrated on proving attacks. Most were targetted at Channel convoys or coastal targets as the Luftwaffe strategists sought to discover the effectiveness and organisation of RAF Fighter Command. In particular they wanted to discover the practical effectiveness of the British radar systems that provided early warnings of incoming German formations.

STUKAS OVER TANGMERE, 1940

This photo shows Stuka divebombers pulling up after dropping thier bombs during a raid on Tangmere during the Battle of Britain. The Stuka was able to deliver its bombs with deadly precision, but was to prove to be highly vulnerable to fighters in aerial combat unless protected by Luftwaffe fighters.

On 9 July A patrol led by Lott ran into a force of six Messerschmitt Bf110s. These big, twin engined fighters were slower and less nimble than the Hurricane, but more heavily armed. The fight was short and sharp, with two German aircraft falling to Lott's guns and a third being badly damaged by another No.43 pilot. However, Lott was badly wounded. He managed to get his men home, but had to bale out of his fighter since it was too shot up to land safely. Lott was taken away in the "meat wagon" to the base medical centre. From there he was taken off to a better equipped hospital, but his wounds proved to be serious and he lost his right eye. Lott never flew in combat again, but he held a succession of command positions before, in 1944, going to Washington as part of the RAF Delegation to the USA. After the war he rose steadily through the ranks to finish his service career as Commandant, School of Land/Air Warfare, with the rank of Air Vice Marshal.

The first real action for No.43 came on 19 July. By this time the squadron was under the command of Squadron Leader John Badger, widely known as "Tubby". Badger was one of the outstanding prewar fighter pilots of the RAF, winning competitions and awards at air shows. He had not, as yet, actually shot down any German aircraft and so was keen to get into action.

The morning had been spent in readiness for attacks on Sussex that never came. All the action was taking place over Kent, and at 4pm a force of German bombers was picked up by radar heading for Dover when all the Kent-based RAF fighters were already busy. No.43 scrambled from Tangmere and raced east to intercept. When they arrived they found themselves outnumbered by more than two to one by a large force of Messerschmitt Bf109 fighters flying escort. Within minutes three Hurricanes were shot down. Two pilots, Flt Lt Simpson and Sgt Crisp baled out, but Sgt Buck was killed. Simpson had already got a bullet through his leg and broke his collarbone on landing, but he discharged himself from hospital 12 days later and headed back to Tangmere. Carey, meanwhile, shot down a 109.

On 21 July the squadron performed a feat that made them world famous, though war time censorship meant that at the time the identity of the squadron concerned was not printed in the newspapers. A convoy of merchant ships was heading up the English Channel for London and had reached Bognor Regis when radar picked up a formation of German aircraft on an intercept course. At Tangmere, Squadron Leader Badger was at readiness along with five other pilots. They were ordered into the air and as their Hurricanes swept out to sea, climbing for height, were given a course to steer that would lead them to the German aircraft. Badger organised his six Hurricanes into two flights of three. He was leading one himself, with Flt Lt Thomas Morgan heading the second. They had not yet reached Bognor and the convoy when Badger spotted the Germans. There was a bombing formation of 40 Dornier Do17 bombers, with a close escort of about 20 Messerschmitt Bf110 twin engined fighters. High overhead was an upper escort of Messerschmitt Bf109 fighters, which Badger thought numbered about two dozen aircraft. The bombers were about 2,000 feet above the Hurricanes, which were now climbing fast.

"Huns ahead, chaps", called Badger over the radio. "It's like looking up at Piccadilly Circus escalator. Line ahead, chaps. Let's upset them a bit." He sent Morgan and his flight to tackle the Bf110s, while he led his wingmen to attack the bombers. Badger opened fire first, at the rather long range of 250 yards, but his aim was good and pieces flew off the Dornier at which he was aiming. Badger then veered to get a second bomber in his sights and fired again, this time knocking out an engine.

Up above, Morgan and his comrades had got in among the Bf110s. Morgan had caused one German to go down with a clearly damaged wing, while another Hurricane pumped bullets into a second German with the result that one of the enemy's engines caught fire. There was no time to celebrate, for now the Bf109 single engined fighters dived down to join the fray.

Morgan spotted a Bf109 on his tail and flipped his aircraft up to try to evade the stream of bullets coming his way. Instantly the entire cockpit cover of Morgan's Hurricane was covered in oil. Assuming his engine oil lines had been severed by the German, Morgan pushed his fighter's nose down and steered north toward land. Unable to see anything through the oil, Morgan flung back the canopy hood and half stood in the cockpit so that his head poked up out of the canopy and he could see where he was going. Finding that the engine still seemed to be running, Morgan headed for Tangmere. When he landed he found that his fighter was totally undamaged, the oil had come from some other aircraft.

Back in the fight, Badger was also hit. A cannon shell hit his port wing and tore off the aileron. He too put his nose down and headed for Tangmere. The other pilots continued the fray, and eight more Germans were seen to be damaged by their gunfire. As each No.43 pilot ran out of ammunition or was damaged he dropped out of the fight and headed for home. Their mission had been successful for the German bombing attack so badly disrupted that the bombs were scattered over a wide range of sea and none of the ships in the convoy were damaged.

What Badger and his men did not know, however, was that soon after they had taken off an RAF staff officer from London had arrived at Tangmere with a journalist from the USA in tow. The journalist had been promised a day at a fighter base, and Tangmere had been chosen almost at random. Escorted by the staff officer, the journalist was shown about the base. He was being led to the control room when Morgan's Hurricane came in to land covered in oil. Soon after that, Badger's fighter came in with a chunk missing from its port wing. The American asked if he could talk to the pilots. The staff officer

HURRICANES REFUELLING AT TANGMERE, 1940
When the Hurricane was first introduced to RAF service it was fuelled by 87 octane aviation fuel, but by the summer of 1940 the aircraft's Merlin engine was being tweaked to run on 100 octane fuel. This gave the Hurricane an extra 35mph of speed and greatly increased its climb rate.

agreed, but said it could only be a quick chat at that point since the pilots had to attend debriefing after which they might be free. The journalist scampered across the grass and hailed Badger.

"How many did you meet?" the American asked.

"Oh," replied Badger tugging off his flying helmet. "About 40 Dorniers, I should say. Plus about the same number of Messerschmitts. Yes, must have been about eighty in all."

"And how many squadrons did you have?' queried the journalist.

Badger laughed. "Not even one. I had six of our boys from No.43. That was enough."

At that point the journalist was hustled away and told he had to wait until the pilots were ready to talk to him at length. Some time later the American was allowed to talk to Badger and Morgan to get the full story, scribbling down details of the battle over Bognor. The story of how six RAF pilots had climbed to attack 80 Luftwaffe aircraft was subsequently splashed across newspapers the length and breadth of the USA, and later was repeated in neutral countries across the world.

The incident proved to be a turning point, for it was the first time that many people in neutral countries realised that Britain really was prepared to fight on alone. In the previous months Poland, Denmark, Norway, Belgium, Holland and even the mighty France had all fallen to the German military machine. Some fighting had been intense, but often the panzers had simply stormed through defences as if they barely existed and then rounded up vast

FLIGHT LIEUTENANT JOHN SIMPSON, 1940
Simpson joined No.43 Squadron as a pilot before the war and remained with the squadron for longer than most of his pre-war comrades. Late in 1940 he was promoted to Squadron Leader and sent to join No.245 Squadron.

numbers of dispirited prisoners too shattered even to fight. Many had expected Britain to go the same way, or to negotiate a hurried peace treaty. Nobody outside Britain had really taken the new Prime Minister Winston Churchill seriously when he had stated the determination of the British to fight it out. Now people began to believe him.

Soon afterwards Morgan was awarded a DFC, the citation stating that "His behaviour in action has been an inspiration to the pilots in his flight."

On 4 August the squadron acquired a rather unusual new pilot in the form of a Belgian with the splendid name of Lt Daniel Albert Raymond George Le Roy du Vivier. He had already had an alarmingly adventurous war. He had served his conscription in the Belgian army from 1935 to 1937, after which he volunteered for the Belgian Air Force and gained his pilot's wings in 1938. He was sent to No.4 Squadron and when the German invasion began on 10 May was at Nivelles. He volunteered to take up a Fairey Firefly reconnaissance aircraft as part of a three aircraft patrol to seek to locate the lead German columns, thought to be somewhere in eastern Brabant. He was then shot down by Belgian troops, who mistook his aircraft for a Messerschmitt, near Keerbergen.

Du Vivier got back to his squadron only to find that it was under orders to evacuate south to evade the advancing German panzers. The squadron moved from base to base, losing men and machines as the fighting grew increasingly desperate. On 28 May King Leopold of Belgium surrendered himself and the ground army fighting in Belgium to the Germans, but urged all Belgians who could do so to escape and continue the war from France or Britain. Du Vivier and his squadron fought on until 19 June. On that day a French army officer arrived to tell them that France had surrendered, and that they all had to surrender as well. The aircraft were disabled and all equipment impounded.

Du Vivier and the nine other surviving pilots quickly decided that since the last orders they had received from their king had been to fight on, they would do so and ignore the French surrender. They fled in the night, hitching rides on trucks and trains heading south. Eventually they reached the Mediterraanean port of Port Vendres. The French port was in turmoil with refugees desperate to get across the sea to French colonies in North Africa, a stream of contradictory orders from different officials in the French government and the German panzers expected to arrive at any moment. Du Vivier and his fellow Belgians found a British merchant ship that was about to depart for Gibraltar and persuaded the captain to let them come on board. They reached Gibraltar on 27 June and were welcomed with open arms by the British.

Du Vivier and his compatriots were quickly transported to Liverpool. They were then moved to a training airfield where they were hurriedly put through a conversion course to learn how to fly Hurricanes and how to use standard RAF radio procedures. It was after completing this hurried course that du Vivier was given the rank of Pilot Officer in the Royal Air Force and bundled off to No.43 Squadron arriving at Tangmere as the fighting was hotting up.

Meanwhile, Simpson had got back to Tangmere in time to join a massed battle over the Isle of Wight on 8 August that saw No.43 Squadron tackle a large force of Stuka divebombers and escorting Messerschmitt Bf109 fighters. This was also du Vivier's first fight with the RAF. No.43 lost six aircraft, with two pilots killed, but shot down 27 Germans and claimed another 18 as damaged. Badger's Hurricane was badly shot up in the fight, though he himself was not injured. He landed back at Tangmere, sprang from his cockpit and ran to a nearby undamaged Hurricane, fired up the engine and took off straight back into action.

On 14 August, No.43 Squadron was scrambled again to head for Kent. They had barely taken off and disappeared off to the east when the air raid sirens wailed at Tangmere. The ominous shape of Stuka divebombers appeared plummeting down from the sky. Soon Tangmere was shuddering to the pounding of bombs that destroyed a hangar, six aircraft and dozens of buildings. A quick radio message recalled No.43, and the Hurricanes tore into action over Tangmere as the last few Stukas were dropping their bombs. The dogfight that followed saw nine Stukas shot down for no loss to No.43. But Tangmere was a wreck.

Next day the Germans were back. More Stukas pummelled the base at 1pm out of a clear sky. The Stukas came down out of the sun without warning, forcing the pilots of No.43 to scramble into the air, dodging the bomb craters left from the previous day's raid while fresh bombs fell around them. Amazingly none of the Hurricanes racing to take off were damaged, but 14 others were destroyed. Among the pilots to get into the air was the Belgian du Vivier. He climbed rapidly, found a Stuka in his sights and fired. The bomber fell from the sky to crash not far from Tangmere. Two more hangars were flattened, along with the Officers' Mess and many other buildings. Nobody at Tangmere knew it at the time, but the Luftwaffe pilots reported that the base had been totally destroyed, so no more raids were made on Tangmere. In fact the base was badly damaged, but not out of action. No.43 continued to fly from Tangmere.

Carey was building up his score of destroyed German aircraft. He got a probable on 12 August and a definite kill on 14 August. He shot down two of the Stukas that bombed Tangmere on 16 August and two days later was leading the squadron into combat when they pounced on a formation of Stukas with a Bf109 escort over Thorney Island. Carey himself got a Stuka before he received a bullet in the leg and had his Hurricane so badly damaged that he had to put it down in a crashlanding near Pulborough. His injuries took him away from No.43 again. By the time he was once more fit for duty,

---

MESSERSCHMITT BF109, 1940
By the time the Battle of Britain began, earlier models of the BF109 had been replaced by the Emil or BF109E. This version had an uprated DB601A engine that increased speed by 30mph and had two cannon slung under the wings. It remained the standard Luftwaffe fighter for over a year.

Carey was sent to fight the Japanese with No.135 Squadron. He fought over Burma and by 1944 had raised his total of known kills to 30 and been awarded two bars to his DFC. After the war he stayed in the RAF to teach fighter tactics to new recruits, but in 1958 took up the post of Air Attache at the British Embassy in Australia. He later worked for Rolls Royce and died in 2004.

Meanwhile, after Carey left, No.43 continued to fight the Battle of Britain. On 12 August there began a concerted series of assaults on RAF air bases near the South Coast. The German aim was to render these bases useless as fighter bases, forcing the Hurricanes and Spitfires further north, away from the Channel overwhich the Luftwaffe sought to gain air superiority.

JUNKERS JU87 STUKAS, 1940
The Stuka was a fiendishly accurate divebomber
that was instrumental in achieving German victories
in the early years of the war, smashing battlefield
targets with ease. However, its slow speed and
limited defensive armament made it easy prey for
RAF fighters unless closely escorted.

No.43 Squadron was joined on 18 August by a young sergeant pilot, and talented engineer, named George Palliser. The new arrival proved to be a popular member of the squadron, but did not stay long before moving on to No.605 Squadron where he was to shoot down 11 enemy aircraft. Palliser was to be one of the most long lived of the Battle of Britain pilots. At the time of writing this in 2011, he is alive and well in Australia.

On 24 August the German assault moved on to RAF bases further north, apparently in the belief that the bases nearer the coast had been so badly damaged that they were incapable of being used for anything other than emergency landings. This was not the case, a failure of Luftwaffe intelligence that allowed the RAF to repair bases such as Tangmere and bring them back up to full operational strength. Not only were bases being repaired, so were aircraft as a system of moving damaged fighters to workshops and civilian airfields for repair or cannibalisation got underway. The RAF's efficient pilot training programme also played a hand as men first called up on the outbreak of war were now emerging from their training schools. Some of these men were woefully inexperienced on the Hurricanes or Spitfires that they flew, but they were competent pilots and were able to be thrown into the battle to ensure that the RAF could field almost as many fighters at its end as when it began.

On 26th August, No.43 were sent up to intercept a raid on Portsmouth – and again ran in to a large force of German fighters. Six Hurricanes were shot down, though all pilots were rescued. Four days later Squadron Leader Badger was shot down. This time his injuries proved to be too severe for him to return to duty, indeed they were to be fatal for he died on 30 June 1941. Badger had accounted for six German raiders during his time in command of No.43.

Command of the squadron passed to Caesar Hull, an outgoing Rhodesian who had been with the squadron when the war broke out and had often flown alongside Townsend in action.

On 2 September the squadron was involved in a large dogfight over Sidcup. The Belgian du Vivier got on the tail of a Messerschmitt Bf109, but was so intent on getting his second kill that he never even saw the German that bounced him from behind. The engine of his Hurricane burst into flames and fire began to lick backward around the cockpit. Du Vivier pushed back the canopy, scrambled out and hurled himself into thin air. He was concerned to find himself only 3,000 feet from the ground, but fortunately his parachute opened in time. He landed in a garden, and was quickly surrounded by a crowd of very noisy and belligerant teenage schoolgirls. Some were brandishing brooms, others hockey sticks and one a fearsome garden fork.

"Are you British?" demanded one of the girls, giving du Vivier a vicious prod with a broom handle. Worried that his poor English and heavy Belgian accent might be mistaken for German, du Vivier decided to play dead. He lay still and began moaning as if badly hurt and semi conscious. After some tense minutes, du Vivier caught sight of a uniform through his half-closed eyes and decided it was time to identify himself. He handed over his identity papers to a suspicious police constable, who quickly ushered the girls away and told a teacher to send for an ambulance. Du Vivier was rushed off to hospital where his burns were cared for. On 22 October he was released and sent back to No.43.

On 4 September Caesar Hull led No.43 Squadron to attack a vast formation of Bf110 fighters over the Sussex coast. In the ensuing dogfight the squadron shot down eight Germans, with Hull getting two himself, for the loss of only one Hurricane. It was a sign of things to come. The RAF pilots had got the measure of the heavily armed, but slow Bf110 and were starting to shoot it down in large numbers. Soon the Luftwaffe would withdraw the Bf110 from its role as a fighter and use it in its secondary roles as a ground-attack aircraft and a nightfighter, in both of which tasks it proved to be highly successful.

Next day the squadron was involved in another large fight, this time over Dungeness. This time the main adversary was the Bf109, though Bf110s and Junkers bombers were also present. Six Germans were shot down, while No.43's only casualty was Tom Morgan who picked up a nasty cut to his face when German bullets smashed his cockpit canopy, but otherwise left his aircraft intact.

Finally, on 6th September, the Luftwaffe switched from attacking RAF bases to bombing cities, towns and factories. Unknown to anyone in Britain a top level German conference attended by Hitler, Goering and others had decided to postpone the invasion of Britain. It was soon to be cancelled as the Germans accepted they could not gain control of the air. Instead the Germans decided to grind down the will and ability of the British to continue the war. Cities were to be bombed by night, both to damage industry and to kill civilians in the hope that this would break their will to fight. Meanwhile, the German navy would use its U-boats and surface raiders to attack convoys and so starve Britain into surrender. Both the navy and the Luftwaffe complained that they did not have the resources to carry out these tasks, and demanded more men and machines. They got neither for Hitler had decided to attack Russia and poured resources into the German army.

On 7th September, No.43 were ordered to be "in readiness" in case they were needed to plug holes left by the squadrons earmarked for action that day. The call came in the later afternoon as they were needed to tackle a large German formation over Folkestone. Ceasar Hull led nine Hurricanes to the attack. He found 25 Dornier Do17 bombers in tight formation with a close escort of Bf109 fighters and a second escort higher up. Hull detailed a flight led by John Kilmartin to tackle the fighters while he led the rest of No.43 to take on the bombers. "Come on, let's smash them up," declared Hull over the radio. Hull shot down two Dorniers, but then the German fighters came down and a dogfight broke out.

Richard Reynell had a Bf109 on his tail, and Hull went down to help him, followed by his own wingman Alan Deller. But a group of prowling Bf109s was lurking in ambush and pounced. All three Hurricanes were shot down, with only Deller managing to bail out and escape alive. Hull's aircraft crashed on the playing fields of a boy's school at Purley, his body inside it. He had been killed by a single bullet through the heart. HIs body was taken back to Tangmere for burial. With Hull's death only three men were left with No.43 who had been in the squadron when the war broke out less than a year before.

Back in Rhodesia the citizens of Hull's home town of Shangani held a

FLIGHT LIEUTENANT JOHN KILMARTIN, 1940
Born in Ireland, Kilmartin went to Australia to work on cattle stations before joining the RAF in 1937. He served with No.43 Squadron twice, once before the war and again during the Battle of Britain, having fought in France with No.1 Squadron in the intervening period.

MESSERSCHMITT BF110, 1941
A rare photograph of a low-flying Bf110 dropping bombs on Britain from a low height. The vulnerability of the Bf110 in fighter battles saw it transfer to a role as a fast, light bomber launching nuisance raids on Britain. Later variants were equipped with air-to-air radar and served as effective nightfighters.

collection and with the proceeds put up a granite obelisk beside the bridge over the River Shangani which carried a brass plaque commemorating Hull and his exploits. In 2003, by which time Rhodesia had become Zimbabwe, the government of Robert Mugabe declared that memorials to white Rhodesians were no longer wanted. The granite obelisk was overturned. A member of the Hull family attempted to retrieve the remains, but was shot at by supporters of Mugabe and fled. The following year a former Rhodesian air force officer managed to extract the brass plaque and sent it to the museum at RAF Tangmere for safety, and there it remains.

The day after Hull was killed, No.43 moved to Usworth, near Sunderland. Eight days later Thomas Morgan was promoted to command the squadron. He had joined the RAF in 1935 and been with No.43 Squadron since the hectic days fighting over Dunkirk. He would command the squadron until early in 1942, gaining a bar to his DFC in May 1941. By the time he stopped combat flying in the summer of 1943, he had accounted for 17 enemy aircraft. He was then seconded to the USAAF 4th Fighter Group to advise on German air tactics and how to counter them. He survived the war and lived until 2004.

On to the Attack

The Battle of Britain was over, but things were not quiet for No.43 Squadron. They moved on to other bases in the north, including Drem and Crail in Scotland over the winter of 1940-41. The squadron at this time welcomed a dashing new arrival in the shape of Flt Lt Colin Gray, a New Zealander who had shot down 14 German aircraft during the Battle of Britain when with No.1 Squadron. Gray did not stay long, less than a month later his old squadron demanded him back as a flight commander. Gray went on to claim 27 kills, plus 6 probables and 12 damaged. He was awarded a DFC and two bars. He would remain in the RAF until 1961, after which he returned to New Zealand to work in industry.

FLIGHT LIEUTENANT COLIN GRAY, 1941
The top-scoring New Zealand ace of the war came to No.43 squadron in the autumn of 1940. Although his stay with the squadron was only brief he did much to raise morale and train new pilots after the losses the squadron suffered in the Battle of Britain. He ended the war with a DSO, and the DFC and two bars.

Another new arrival in Scotland was the newly qualified pilot Raymond Harries. Harries proved to be an exceptional pilot, and in the spring of 1941 was taken away from No.43 Squadron to become a pilot instructor. He returned to combat later in the war, downing 15 German aircraft and a V1. He was awarded the DSO and Bar, DFC and bar and the Belgian Croix de

FOCKE WULF FW190, 1942

When the FW190 appeared in combat over France early in 1941 it came as a nasty shock to the RAF who had no idea that the Germans had been working on a new fighter. It easily outperformed the latest models of Spitfire. The Germans built 4,677 of this FW190A and later produced a number of uprated variants building 20,051 in all.

Guerre. He was killed in 1950 when his Meteor fighter crashed accidentally in Yorkshire.

Finally there came to the squadron Mohinder Singh, one of 18 Indian pilots who had volunteered for the RAF. he later wrote of his time with the squadron "I was attached with No.43 Squadron, flying Hurricanes from Martlesham, the RAF fighter Squadrons being switched from base to base every few weeks, but remaining in the Greater London area. Later, we converted to the Spitfire Mk.V and I was promoted to Flight Commander. Our operational task now included fighter sweeps over occupied Europe and we made low-level attacks on enemy targets when we were not required to provide fighter escort to RAF bombers. During these operations, I was involved in many dog fights with Luftwaffe fighters and my total tally was two Messerschmitt Bf109s confirmed as shot down and three damaged". Singh later served in India against the Japanese and after the war became an airline pilot.

With the focus of the war shifting away from the air fighting over Britain, No.43 Squadron enjoyed a rather quiet time. There were many patrols to be flown and efforts were made to catch the German bombers operating at night, but compared to the hectic summer of 1940 there was little actual fighting.

This does not mean that there was a lack of trouble, much of it caused by one Pilot Officer Thomas Fletcher. Fletcher had joined the squadron stright from pilot training and soon managed to rub almost everyone up the wrong way. Arguments and disputes were frequent, with the squadron commander being particularl prone to argue with Fletcher. In the end, Fletcher was forcibly transferred to Coastal Command where he began flying a Walrus flying boat on air-sea rescue missions. On 2 October 1942 Fletcher was sent to rescue a Spitfire pilot from the Channel, but arrived to find the man's dinghy in the middle of a minefield and being shelled by German artillery. Nothing daunted, Fletcher went down while his Spitfire escort fought off a squadron of Messerschmitt Bf109 fighters that had come down to attack the slow Walrus. Despite a choppy sea, Fletcher rescued the pilot and took off under fire. His commanding officer at once recommended him for a Victoria Cross, writing "Sergeant Fletcher was fully aware of the risks involved when he volunteered for the task. He carried out the rescue with conspicuous gallantry... he ignored all dangers, and through coolness, considered judgment and skill succeeded in picking up the pilot." In the event Fletcher was awarded a DFM, gaining a bar three months later when he rescued a downed German crew in appallingly heavy seas. Fletcher ended the war having saved more men than any other air-sea rescue pilot. He seemed to have got over his early poor temper for he remained in the RAF after the war as a popular officer and retired in 1964.

Other pilots managed to get on at No.43 rather more successfully. The Belgian du Vivier, for instance, had finally got his second confirmed kill, a Junkers Ju88 light bomber, and in January 1942 had been awarded the DFC. He had also risen to the position of a flight commander and was proving to be a popular and effective leader.

The squadron was re-equipped with the Hurricane Mk IIC, a slower but much more heavily armed variant of the fighter. The IIC carried four 20mm cannon it its wings to replace the eight machine guns, but also up to 500lb of bombs slung under the wings. This made it a formidable ground attack machine, the squadron reverting to the role that it had made its own in the Great War. In July 1942 the squadron was suddenly shifted back to its old base in Sussex. As events were to prove the move back to Tangmere was for a very specific purpose.

On 12 August 1942 the gates to RAF Tangmere were locked shut and all leave cancelled. There followed a series of intense preparations and top secret opertional briefings. On 19 August some 6,000 men, most of them Canadians, were landed on the coast of France at Dieppe. The ostensible reason for the large scale raid was to seize and destroy the port and assorted military installations nearby. The real reason was, however, to test tactics and equipment devised by the Allies for assaulting an enemy-held coastline.

The raid proved to be a costly enterprise. Almost 60% of the men who landed at Dieppe were killed, wounded or captured. The tanks in particular proved to be unsuited to amphibious operations and the landing craft failed to deliver men to where they were supposed to go. The best that can be said is that the heavy Canadian casualaties at Dieppe saved thousands more Allied lives in future amphibious attacks on Sicily, Italy and Normandy.

In the air, the Dieppe Raid was quite diffeerent. The RAF had been tasked with gaining and holding for 24 hours total air control over the combat area. This they managed to do, though towards dusk the concerted attacks by German fighter squadrons were taking a heavy toll on the RAF fighters. No.43 Squadron with their heavily armed Hurricane IICs were give the task of attacking German gun emplacements from low level.

Leading No.43 into Dieppe was the Belgian du Vivier. The first mission of the day proved to be the most hazardous, attacking German beach defences at dawn from very low level to clear the way for the troops landing at Dieppe. The squadron had left Tangmee at 4.25am, and roared into action at just after 5am. As the aircraft tore in low over the sea, they passed over the landing craft heading inshore. Heavy bombers were pounding the hills around the town and were dropping smoke canisters inshore to spoil the aim of German anti-aircraft gunners. At first all seemed fairly peaceful, but as No.43 got to within 500 yards of the coast, dozens of guns opened up at them. Tracer and flak came hurtling up at the Hurricanes as they pushed on into the curtain of fire. One of the Hurricanes was shot down, then the fighters were shooting up their targets before racing over the town's rooftops and heading for the smoke cover over the hills. Emerging from the smoke, the Hurricanaes were attacked by a force of FW190 fighters and a savage dogfight ensued.

Leading one section on this dangerous initial low level attack was one of the more heavily decorated pilots to serve with No.43 Squadron. Frederick Lister was an acting Flight Lieutenant at the time, though he would go on to achieve higher rank. Lister led his section in an attack that he pushed home with great valour and determination. His reward was to see the target badly hit, but also to find that his own Hurricane was peppered with flak damage, and had lost some of its hydraulics. He nevertheless led his section back to base, allowing them to land before he attempted what he knew would be a difficult and possibly fatal landing himself. The landing ended in a smash, from which Lister was lucky to walk away uninjured. Shrugging off the incident, Lister ordered a reserve aircraft to be got ready for his next mission, due later that day. The wreckage was, as was customary, stripped of reuseable items. The undamaged engine was winched out and taken to a workshop.

While Lister was off leading his section on a second attack – they were to make four that day – a reporter from the local newspaper was escorted around the airfield so that he could write up the events for the local people who would have seen the frantic activity of aircraft coming and going all day. When he came across the wreck of Lister's Hurricane he asked whose it was, to be told that it belonged to a pilot who was now back up in the air in a different aircraft. The journalist took a photo that he later had published under the immortal headline of "Pilot Flies Home Without Engine". Lister was later awarded a DFC for his actions that day.

Lister later commanded No.152 Squadron, but it was an incident during his time in command of No.127 squadron that earned him lasting fame in the RAF. He took command in October 1944 when the squadron was based in France and was flying low, ground attack missions over the Western Front. He took up his post and began rebuilding the squadron after heavy losses. He was then shot down and badly injured in the arm. His place at No.127 Squadron was taken by a Czech named Smik, who was himself shot down and killed in December 1944.

Lister was by then recovered from his wounds so he hurried back to No.127 Squadron. He burst into the dispersal hut where the pilots were gathered talking about the loss of Smik. "As I was saying before I was so rudely interrupted," began Lister before being swamped by his pilots. Lister remained in the RAF after the war, being awarded a DSO for his service. He first flew Hawker Hunters and then retrained to command a missile battery. He married in 1957 and retired from the RAF ten years later due to ill health. He died in 1995.

Du Vivier and No.43 Squadron went back to Dieppe three more times that day. As a result of the action, and his determined leadership, du Vivier was awarded a bar to his DFC. "The successes achieved by this squadron, particularly during the Dieppe operations, can be attributed largely to Suadron Leader Le Roy du Vivier's masterly influence and outstanding leadership," read the citation for the DFC bar.

After Dieppe, No.43 Squadron was re-equipped with Spitfires and took to flying aggressive sweeps over northern France. Among their casualties, on 22 September, was the gallant du Vivier who suddenly collapsed and had to be taken away on a stretcher. He was found to be suffering from total fatigue. It was not to be the end of the war for du Vivier, however. In April 1943 he returned to duty to take up a post at the Middle East Command HQ and thereafter held a number of senior staff positions in the RAF Mediterranean command. After the war he would go into the oil industry, but volunteered to spend weekends giving lessons in combat to trainee pilots in the Belgian Air Force. He died in a car crash in 1981.

In November 1942 the squadron was moved from Britain for the first time, to go to North Africa. The campaign fought back and forth across the roasting heat of the North African desert had been going on since 1940 when the Italians had invaded Egypt from their colony of Libya. By the time No.43 Squadron arrived, the Italians and their allies the Germans were commanded by the wily Field Marshal Erwin Rommel. However, Rommel was now in retreat having lost the 2nd Battle of El Alamein to the British under General Bernard Montgomery.

The long German retreat across North Africa was to be interrupted by frequent rallies and counterattacks as Rommel used the terrain and his meagre resources to hit back hard and fast whenever he had the opportunity. No.43 Squadron spent these gruelling months as part of the Western Desert Air Force under Air Vice Marshal Arthur Cuningham. No.43 Squadron operated from a succession of temporary, tented bases as the tide of war shifted inexorably westward from Egypt across Libya into Tunisia.

By February 1943 it was clear that achieving Allied victory in North Africa was only a matter of time, so the Allies began a major restructuring of their forces as they began looking forward to the next move. No.43 Squadron was

SQUADRON LEADER EUGENIUSZ HORBACZEWSKI, 1943
Horbaczewski served with No.43 for most of 1943. He later commanded the all-Polish No.315 Squadron. The exact circumstances of his death in combat with FW190 fighters over France on 18 August 1944 have never been solved.

moved into the newly created No.322 Wing of the renamed Desert Air Force.

The squadron's arrival in Africa was to prove rather dicey. They were shipped to Gibraltar by sea and there presented with new aircraft, Hurricane IIC ground attack fighters. The aircraft were not actually new, but were reconditioned veterans of some months of combat and in some cases were seriously under par. The new commanding officer, Sqdn Ldr Michael Rook may have been relieved that the air officer on Gibraltar looking after the squadron was none other than John Simpson, now promoted to be a Wing Commander, but the orders he received cannot have filled him with joy. The squadron was to fly over the Mediterranean toward the Luftwaffe base at

WING COMMANDER BARRIE HEATH, 1944
Heath joined No.43 Squadron in 1944 and soon the squadron was based in France where their badge earned them the name of "Les Coqs Anglais". By this date the squadron was engaged mostly on ground attack duties.

Mainson Blanche to aid the assault on Algiers. The ground troops attacking Maison Blanche were to send up a signal if they had secured the airfield so that No.43 Squadron could land, but otherwise the Hurricanes were to divert elsewhere.

On 8 November the squadron set off, accompanied by two senior officers Wing Commander Michael Pedley and Group Captain Edwardes-Jones, both in Hurricanes. As No.43 arrived over Maison Blanche there was no sign of the prearranged signal. However, all appeared quiet, so Rook went down to have a look. After a couple of slow passes, Rook thought that the place appeared to be in Allied hands, so he landed and was most relieved to find that he was correct. In fact the defenders had not bee completely overcome, and it was the arrival of the Hurricanes and their slow circling overhead that persuaded the remaining Germans to surrender.

Rommel left Africa in March due to ill health and his place was taken by the Italian General Giovanni Messe. Starved of fuel, ammunition and reinforcements, Messe surrendered on 13 May. There then followed intense debate as to where the large Allied armies in North Africa would strike next. Greece was favoured by some as a way to attack the back door of the German army in Russia, but the terrain there was thought too difficult for rapid movement. Southern Italy offered the chance to knock Italy out of the war, but the sea routes passed too many islands held by German and Italian forces for that to be a safe prospect. Similar considerations ruled out an attack on southern France. In the end the target turned out to be Sicily, which was intended to be a stepping stone on the way to Italy.

In July 1943, the squadron took part in Operation Husky, the invasion of Sicily. They were now part of No.324 Wing. With Sicily secured, the squadron moved to mainland Italy and began a slow crawl up the peninsula moving from base to base as the armies advanced in the face of determined German resistance. The squadron was now commanded by Squadron Leader Eugeniusz Horbaczewski, one of only three Poles commanding RAF squadrons.

Horbaczewski had been born in Kiev at a time when most of Poland was part of the Tsarist Russian Empire, but his family moved to Poland when that country became indpendent after World War I. He qualified as a glider pilot when still at school and joined the Polish air force but had not yet been assigned to a combat squadron when Germany invaded in September 1939. Following orders, Horbaczewski fled through Romania and Greece to Britain where he joined the RAF. After retraining on Spitfires, and learning enough English to understand radio jargon, Horbaczewski entered combat. By the time he came to No. 43 squadron in May 1943 he had already shot down 9 enemy aircraft, and been downed himself once.

Horbaczewski led No.43 Squadron until October, during which time the squadron was involved with the invasions of both Sicily and Italy, and in heavy fighting over Malta. Horbaczewski himself shot down three German FW190 fighters during these months.

By this date the squadron was flying the Spitfire Mk IX. This model was a great improvement on the earlier versions, having a top speed of 408mph and a ceiling of 43,000 feet. It also packed an awesome punch being armed with two 20mm cannnon and either four .303in machine guns or twin .5in machine guns. It could also carry up to 1000lb of bombs. The Spitfire IX was an awesome ground attack fighter, and a useful combat aircraft as well.

In August 1944 the squadron was moved to Ramatuelle in France as the Allies landed at the mouth of the Rhone and began to push north towards Germany. By September they were at Lyon and on 9 September Wing Commander Barrie Heath led the squadron on a sortie into German air space. Heath had joined the squadron with a reputation for a fiery temper and combat success. After the war, Heath left the RAF to enter business and later earned a knighthood for his services to export earnings.

Horbaczewski left No.43 when it went back to Italy and took command of No.315, an exclusively Polish squadron then based in Britain. He shot down five more German fighters and four V1 flying bombs before he went missing on 18 August during a mission over France. His body was found in the remains of his fighter in 1947 and he was given a full military funeral.

The squadron then moved back to Italy, where it remained until the end of the war. After a visit to Austria over the summer of 1945, the squadron was disbanded in 1947.

Into the Jet Age

In February 1949, No.43 Squadron was again formed. They were now back at Tangmere flying Gloster Meteors, the RAF's first operational jet fighters.

The early marks of Meteor were not a huge improvement on the piston-engined fighters, having a top speed of 415mph, which was actually slower than the more advanced versions of the Spitfire. However, the jet engine was not to be denied and was soon delivering massively improved performance. By the time No.43 Squadron was flying Meteors they could hit 600mph without too much trouble. The Meteor was equipped with four 20mm cannon, and could carry up to 16 rockets for attacking ground targets, though these were not always fitted. In 1950 the squadron moved to RAF Leuchars in Scotland. There the squadron received its first formal standard from the Queen as the RAF began to emulate the army in the carrying of unit flags.

GLOSTER METEOR, 1950

No.43 Squadron flew Meteors for four years. In all the aircraft equipped 62 RAF squadrons at one time or another and was sold to 18 foreign air forces. Despite this widespread use, the aircraft had a number of safety issues and and went out of production in 1954.

In 1954 the squadron handed in its Meteors in favour of the Hawker Hunter. This nimble single seat fighter would later be developed into ground attack variants. Able to reach 715mph (Mach 0.94), the Hunter was fast and could reach 50,000 feet in altitude. It was, however, of a very short range since its fuel tanks were small. After a number of crashes caused by running out of fuel, larger tanks were installed and the Hunter became a top class fighter. It was armed with four 30mm cannon and had the ability to carry a range of rockets and bombs. Equipped with the Hunter, No.43 Squadron operated from Cyprus and Aden through the later 1950s and 1960s. It was again disbanded in November 1967.

It was at this time that Flt Lt John Howe joined the squadron as a flight commander. Howe received the Queen's Commendation for Valuable Service while with the squadron before leaving in 1960 to take command of No.74 Squadron. Howe went on to command the Royal Observer Corps, which he thoroughly overhauled, and the RAF Regiment. He would eventually retired with the rank of Air Vice Marshal.

HAWKER HUNTERS, 1955
Four No.43 Squadron Hawker Hunters with their distinctive chequerboard markings. The Hunter entered service with the RAF in 1954 as a highly manoeuvrable sub-sonic jet fighter. It remained in service to the 1970s and was a major export success for the British air industry.

In 1963 the squadron saw action in Aden. That small colony had been acquired by treaty in 1838, and during the 1950s the British prepared the colony for independence despite the fact that Communist Yemen claimed the city and colony for itself. The reulting Aden Emergency, as the small war became known, saw various local groups fighting each other and the British for dominance. No.43 Squadron had the task of flying air operations in support of the Army in the Radfan Mountains. One pilot engaged on these operations was William Stoker, who was awarded the Queen's Commendation for Valuable Service for his actions.

The variety of missions that No.43 Squadron was called upon to carry out was wide. They had to fly patrols along the border between Aden and Yemen to watch for any troop or supply movements being made by the enemy. They had to carry out a large number of attack missions to destroy sites identified by intelligence as being enemy supply dumps or troop resting bases. Finally they were called up at short notice to bomb enemy troops engaged in combat with British or Adenese troops. One veteran of 43 Squadron commented: "We were laying down fire as close as 25 yards to [friendly] army positions."

One pilot who attracted attention flying on these hazardous missions was Flt Lt David Malin. His eye for precision targetting was to become legendary, on one occassion hitting and destroying an individual house from his speeding Hunter. On another mission he was sent to target a Yemeni infantry force that had got a British patrol pinned down in the mountains. Despite having to find his target in a narrow wadi, Malin hit with such accuracy that he inflicted 75% casualties on the enemy. On the ground Malin was noticeable for the fact that he did not immeditaely slope off to relax when off duty. Instead he took the time to pass on his knowledge and skills to newer and less experienced pilots. As the mission to Aden drew to a close, Malin was awarded a much deserved DFC.

The squadron was reformed in September 1969, now being equipped with the McDonnel-Douglas Phantom. This two seater aircraft could operate as a fighter or as a ground attack aircraft. It was able to reach 1,472mph (Mach 2.2) and boasted a ceiling of over 60,000 feet. It had a variety of external hardpoints on to which could be fitted up to 18,600lb of weaponry, including rockets, missiles and cannon.

No.43 Squadron kept its Phantoms until 1989 when it acquired the Tornado F3. The Tornado was designed to be a long range interceptor, not a close combat fighter, so it had an impressive combat range of more than 1,150 miles and could remain airbourne for more than two hours. Its speed was comparable to the Phantom and it could carry an on board 20mm revolving cannon as well as a wide variety of missiles attached to 10 external hardpoints. It was with the Tornado that the squadron fought in the Gulf War of 1991.

On 2 August 1990 Iraq invaded Kuwait without warning and within two days had conquered that small oil-rich state on the Persian Gulf. Much of the Kuwaiti airforce and the royal family managed to escape to Saudi Arabia. There then followed months of diplomatic activity aimed at getting the Iraqi dictator Saddam Hussein to pull out of Kuwait, but to no avail. Other Arab states and Western Powers were alarmed by both the increase in Iraqi power and by Iraqi belligerance. A coalition was put together under United Nations authority to restore independence to Kuwait.

No.43 Squadron was part of the contribution made by Britain. They were stationed in Saudi Arabia and played a full role in Operation Instant Thunder, as the air component of the war to oust the Iraqis from Kuwait was called. The British air commanders were Air Vice-Marshal Andrew Wilson (to 17 November) and Air Vice-Marshal Bill Wratten (from 17 November), the British squadrons raided deep into Iraq to hit military and infrastructure targets.

In 1994 the squadron flew to Gioia del Colle in southern Italy to take part in Operation Deny Flight, the enforcement of a No Fly Zone over Bosnia, in what had been Yugoslavia, but was now a complicated mass of warring mini states. The role of No.43 was to fly gruelling four hour patrols over Yugoslavia to watch for any aircraft breaking the No Fly Zone. If one were spotted, the British pilots had first to radio the aircraft that they were breaking the zone, then radio back to base for instructions. Inevitably it took so long for any action to be authorised that the offending intruder had completed its mission before the British pilots were authorised to do anything about it. It was a frustrating time for No.43 pilots.

On 22 September, No.43 finally took part in a real mission. They provided fighter cover for a Jaguar of No.41 Squadron sent to destroy a Serb T55 tank that was breaching a cease fire agreement. The tank was destroyed without trouble and No.41 Squadron were dubbed "The Can Openers" by their colleagues on Operation Deny Flight. It was the first time that a bomb had been dropped in anger in Europe since 1945.

Back in Britian, No.43 Squadron earned some very public headlines when Helen Gardiner became the first female RAF pilot to intercept a Russian

TORNADO F3, 2001

The Tornado was designed to be a long-range
interceptor, tasked with tackling Soviet bombers
heading from Britain from the Arctic and over the
North Sea. This No.43 Squadron aircraft shows both
the cock badge and the black and white chequers
on the tail.

spy plane on September 10 1996. She was flying out of RAF Leuchars at the
time. Three years later, Gardiner went on to become the first female pilot to
fly 1000 hours in a fast jet.

In 2003, No.43 Squadron returned to Iraq to fight in the Iraq War when
an alliance led by the USA and Britain invaded Iraq to overthrow Saddam
Hussein. The British element of the war went by the name of Operation
Telic and had as its objective the city of Basra and surrounding lands. The
RAF units were commanded by Air Vice Marshal Glenn Torpy, and had as
their principal task clearing the way for the ground forces heading for Basra.
No.43 Squadron was operating out of Prince Sultan in Saudi Arabia alongside
No.111 Squadron, which also had Tornado F3 aircraft.

On 13 July 2009, No.43 Squadron stood down yet again. The final parade
was held at RAF Leuchars and presided over by Air Chief Marshal Sir Roger
Palin KCB OBE MA FRAeS FIPM RAF, a former commander of the
squadron. Palin gave a speech which concluded "And so, as this Disbandment
Parade draws to a close and as our Squadron Standard, received from Her
Majesty herself here at Leuchars 21 years ago, is marched off for the last time
for now, I wish all of you, individually and collectively, God Speed in your
new endeavours, and we all await the day when the Fighting Cock resumes
its natural status as Cock o' the North. Gloria Finis."